FAITH, FAILURE, SUCCESS

Stories along the entrepreneurial journey

SAMANTHA DANIELLE   **LEONARD MOGUL**

PIERRE DEBOIS   **GLENN MURRAY**

OLIVIA DEMOSS   **MEL ROBERSON**

Cover Design: Janie Lee

Interior Design: Janie Lee

Published by: 220 Publishing

Faith, Failure, Success: Stories Along the Entrepreneurial Journey. Samantha Danielle, Pierre DeBois, Olivia DeMoss, Leonard Mogul, Glenn Murray, Mel Roberson. First Edition.

ISBN: 978-1-5136-6367-8

ACKNOWLEDGEMENTS

Thank you:
God.
Cleatrice.
Rheuben Jr.
Yolanda.
Jaclyn.
Ali.
Glenn.
And last but not least, I'd like to thank myself.

— *Samantha Danielle*

If you live long enough in life you are blessed to have many chapters. For my business chapter I am grateful for everyone—family, friends, and partners—who has supported my progress along this entrepreneurial way. A special thank you goes to my mom, B. Lucille DeBois. I love you.

— *Pierre DeBois*

My entire life has changed because I have the honor of being called dad by two incredible young women. To my daughters Alayna and Raelyn, you are my reasons for existing. Also, thanks to my family, friends, and mentors who have supported me long the way. Lastly, my parents and my brother who have always been there for me.

— *Mel Roberson*

Thanks to the team at 220 Publishing for their dedication and hard work on this project (Stephanie Reynolds, Janie Lee, Justin McMullen). The contributors (Sam, Mel, Leonard, Pierre, Olivia). Latresa Rice for the Foreword. All the quote contributors (amazing job!).

This book is dedicated to my family: Robert, Delores, Dee, Katrina, Krissy, Rod, Tony, Kia, Mike, Thomas, Tristen and Anthony. The God Kids! Klynn, Iman and Bryson. And I dedicate this book to the memory of my mom, Joyce Murray. And special thanks to all along the way who taught me the meaning of having faith, being humble in my success and understanding that failure is not final.

— Glenn Murray

A special thank you to all of the quote contributors: Jennifer Christenson, Johnnita Robinson, Cortez Mack, Alisa Inez, Shari C. Hill, Tangee Moscoso, Mary Stowers, Dee Stokes, Cynda Williams, Christine E. Burlison, Connie Glover, Tammy Lyn Connors, Keisha Rose, Robert Hazzard, Mona McIlwain, Toni Nicole, James L. Papandrea and Anthony Ellis McGee.

TABLE OF CONTENTS

FOREWORD

Faith is belief and trust in God, to the extent that it causes failure to be a place-marker instead of your final destination. God has given us all things that pertain to life and how to reflect His image in the earth through our personal lives and businesses. Although we are not God, we can be "like" Him. For example, He is omniscient, meaning He knows everything about us and this world. Entrepreneurs who are doing their best to be "like" God in their business research their competition, know their clients, research effective marketing techniques to reach those clients and execute the plans consistently. You have to know your industry and clients well so that when you "share the good news" about your products (solutions to their problems), they will pay to receive them.

Just like God is omniscient, He is also omnipotent, meaning He has all power. Entrepreneurs who are doing their best to be "like" God operate from the mindset of, "If I can think it, then it is already done. I'm just taking the steps in the natural to see the physical manifestation of what has already been accomplished." These entrepreneurs believe that nothing is impossible for them. Sometimes they may feel afraid; but they embrace the challenges and pursue their dreams despite all the barriers they encounter in the process.

Last but not least, God is omnipresent, meaning He is in all places at all times. Entrepreneurs who are doing their best to be "like" God diversify their marketing strategy. These entrepreneurs know the importance of branding. They are seen wearing their brand frequently, talking about it, posting about it on various social media outlets, writing blogs using it, participating on panels and other face to face networking outlets. They market their brand so effectively that people who they have never met feel like they know them personally. When your brand is everywhere, so are you.

Although we can never be God, we are called to be like him as business professionals. Failure is never our final destination; it's one step in our process to obtaining our dreams. Everyone wants to be successful. To me, success means consistently doing the things that you love, while simultaneously being paid well and having the time to do them. You cannot be successful without failure. When a child is attempting to walk, they typically fall at least once. Once that child falls, the parent normally will watch the child to see if the child gets back up and tries to walk again without assistance. The parent never gives up on that child's dream of walking just like God never gives up on us when we fall during our Christian walk. If you have fallen in your personal life or in your business, make the choice to get back up. Faith and failure are the business partners that will lead you to success.

—Latresa Rice, Spiritual Leader/Author
Gate to Life; Fruit Circle

FAITH

Faith is an enormous word because its meaning encompasses so much. For a long time, I thought faith was just about believing in God, myself or another, but what I've found is that belief is not enough. Faith has to do with absolutely knowing. There is no room for doubt when I truly have faith. If I know God is going to provide for my needs, I don't have to have the "thing" in my sights. Before it manifests, I have to grasp it within—the touch, the smell, the sight, the taste, and the joy it brings me before it comes. That kind of conviction takes practice. There are very few instances where I've just known something to be true if I couldn't use my earthly senses to perceive it. I find that my faith in certain people is more ingrained. Because I witness them and their actions, I know who they are to me. I can discern if they deserve my faith or not. Honestly, I have been working on having faith in myself for years. Our culture rarely conditions children to believe in themselves. Young ones think that adults have all the answers. They are not taught to listen to their voice within. I have found that I have to consciously discipline myself to clear my mind, hear my own inner voice and trust it. Every time I do, it rarely lets me down.

—Cynda Williams

THE MASK

by Samantha Danielle

Love is patient, love is kind. It does not envy, it does not boast, it is not proud. It does not dishonor others, it is not self-seeking, it is not easily angered, it keeps no record of wrongs. Love does not delight in evil but rejoices with the truth. It always protects, always trusts, always hopes, always perseveres. **Love never fails**.

— 1 Corinthians 4-8

Don't react off love. **F love**. *Come out of the situation and look at it third person...for what it really is and then make a decision... because love is so blind.*

— Robyn Fenty, ABC News Interview

As a former wedding planner, the above two quotes deeply resonated with me. I executed numerous weddings while silently questioning if I still even believed in true love, much less marriage. This is my story along with some advice on what it takes to maintain a business while, even if for a moment, you struggle with believing in its core value.

WHY LOVE?

1987: As a child who witnessed domestic violence, I had no personal reference for what a healthy marriage looked like between a couple. I have no memories of my parents ever saying "I love you" to each other, celebrating an anniversary or taking a vacation without me. What I do know is that each of them made sure I was given advantages outside of the home to flourish as a child and that has been instrumental in every success I've had as an adult. My parents separated when I was ten years old and my mom moved me and my brother from New York to North Carolina.

1995: While I had friends in high school whose parents had been together for a while, I didn't spend a lot of "family time" with them. It wasn't until college that I had repeated close encounters with couples who had been together since before their children were born. There were the couples who embarrassed their kids on move-in day when they high-fived each other and exclaimed, "Freedom!!" about being empty nesters. There were couples who publicly and unashamedly hugged and kissed. The couples who openly and repeatedly said "I love you" touched me the most. This is when I fell in love with love.

1999-2001: I graduated from East Carolina University in 1999 with a Bachelor of Science in Nursing. With the goal of becoming a pediatric hospital administrator, I immediately enrolled in graduate school. In 2001, I earned a Master's in Business Administration with a concentration in Healthcare Management. It was in graduate school that I realized how much I enjoyed and excelled in Project Management.

2003: I planned my own wedding and afterwards, my desire to run a pediatric hospital went right out the door. I decided, instead, that I wanted to become a wedding planner. Planning and executing a ceremony and reception is project management at its finest; adding love to that made this the perfect career for me. This was my "why".

2005: Who goes from dolling out pediatric doses of Benadryl to bustling gowns overnight? This woman! While I enjoyed planning my own wedding, there was so much about the industry that I didn't understand. So, I enrolled in a wedding planning certification course and became engrossed with learning about the rules and traditions of weddings. After that, I started advertising with a national wedding magazine and joined a networking group that focused on providing business education to catering and special event professionals.

2009-2012: The three years before the finalization of my divorce is when I wore 'The Mask'.

WEARING THE MASK

My mask is my smile. The very first compliment I remember receiving came from Ms. Marsha. She was an older member at Faith & Victory Church in Greenville, NC, and one day in the parking lot she told me I had the "prettiest smile". I cannot count the number of times I've heard those exact same words since.

This, coupled with my sense of humor, created a bubble around me. My industry peers had no clue that my marriage was ending. In the early years of my business, I cried tears of joy at weddings for many different reasons. Happiness that I did good work and got my couples to the altar. Admiration when witnessing the moment the groom saw his bride and shed a tear. Father of the bride toasts. So forth and so on. Years later, the tears were still there; however, my clients and staff thought they were still about these moments. *Absolutely not.*

I'd lost my enthusiasm for securing new clientele and wasn't inspired by anything they said about what they dreamed of for their wedding day. My creativity was gone, right along with my imagination. I went from having middle of the night epiphanies for event design to staring mindlessly at Shawn T's Insanity Workout infomercials.

From a business perspective, the reason I chose to "wear the mask" was because I didn't want my clients to worry or have any concern that my personal problems would interfere with their wedding day. Simply put, most couples planning a wedding don't really care about other people's problems during that time. They're not heartless; it's just that this is a huge milestone in most people's lives and there's a lot of pressure for it to be a perfect moment in their story.

From a personal perspective, I didn't want to share what was going on with too many family or friends because I was raised where "what happens in the home, stays in the home". Honestly, I didn't want people to look at either one of us differently for the rest of our lives just because we had a rough patch. By the time I broadly shared the news, it was over.

MAINTAINING THROUGH THE MASK

So how did I push through when everything in my personal life seemed to be falling apart? Let me share five things that helped me: remembering why I started the business, talking to God, my team, having an industry peer I could trust and seeking counseling from a therapist. And it took each one of these things to get me through.

1. My "Why"

One of the huge mistakes people make is that they try to force an interest on themselves. You don't choose your passions; your passions choose you.

— Jeff Bezos, Amazon Founder

If not the first, the question of why you want to start your business should be at the top of your list when you are deciding whether or not to become an entrepreneur. You may have heard this before and I am here to tell you it's true: If your why is simply and only to get rich quick, the service industry is probably not for you. It's perfectly fine to have financial goals that result in wealth, but you need to believe, with your entire being, that your product or service fulfills a real need in your target customer's life.

When your ROI goes from negative to break even to marginal for approximately 3-5 years, it's easy to give up on your dreams. The entrepreneurs who achieve the business trifecta (financial gain, time freedom and firing their boss) obtain it after a period of struggle, grind and sacrifice. You quit your Monday-Friday 9a-5a just to end up working Sunday-Saturday 6a-11p. Building a business is one of the most demanding things a person can do. Get ready for the long haul!

2011: I remember once standing at the back of a ceremony and thinking, "F this. Hurry up and get through these fake ass vows so we can get to the party." I'm pretty sure if a camera was aimed on my face, it would have probably showed a look of admiration. Sign me up for an academy award! It was after that wedding that I pondered if I should and could continue in the industry. At that time, I felt sadness at the thought of closing shop. Instead of doing that, I moved from North Carolina to Chicago in 2012 and sought a new business there. The new market was invigorating, and I found real joy again in the profession.

Know this: When the bad times come in your personal life and you can push through, you know your *why* is *real*. You just might have to find a way to rejuvenate and/or refresh yourself. It doesn't have to be as drastic as moving into a new market. You may simply just need to attend an industry conference. Or take a vacation!

2. My Faith

There's a story in Mark 9 about a father who asked Jesus to heal his son. He was broken-hearted that his son had this problem. He was so desperate and pleaded to Jesus as a last resort. Jesus said to him that, "everything is possible for one who believes... And straightway the father of the child cried out, and said with tears, 'Lord, I believe; help thou mine unbelief.'" The worried father pleaded with Jesus to *help* him to have the greater faith demanded of him.

Simply put, trusting in God can be imperfect. It's OK to admit that. The presence of trust doesn't mean that there is an absence of doubt and fear. As a Christian, I understand God gave me a choice. My options were to trust Him to help me find my way back to happiness or continue to wallow in disappointment. I was honest with God. I wanted to still believe in long-lasting love, so I kept saying *it* until I meant *it* again. What was *it* that I kept saying? "I love love!"

3. My Team

I had three 1099 junior planners and a social media assistant. Without them, Bliss by Sam would have been closed before I even moved to Chicago. Because I had implemented processes and procedures for how my company did weddings, there was really no interruption within the business. What I termed the "BBS Way" was documented in an Operations Manual. Here's a snapshot of my corporate culture:

CORPORATE CULTURE

BBS has a wonderful culture - a culture that values each team member's unique skill set and contribution; a culture that is market-focused. BBS rewards superb performance and encourages entrepreneurial thinking. All in all, it is a culture that encourages productive, creative and collaborative work.

Our walk, talk and general demeanor should always be reflective of our corporate culture known as "The BBS Way" which means each team member should be committed to being:
- Educated
- Aware of current trends
- Precise
- Organized
- Timely
- Able to solve problems quickly
- Fun!

1

I moved to Chicago without telling any of my North Carolina staff that I had left. For one, I had clients to still take care of that I didn't want to pass to another planner. I was going back to North Carolina so often that it was easy to pretend I still lived there. This was intentional. I wanted to see if Bliss by Sam was Bliss By Sam without Sam. After about six months, I finally told them about the divorce and the move. They were completely shocked! But in in the end, my theory was right, and it made me happy to know that I'd built a wonderful team who could sustain my business model without me.

If you're an entrepreneur starting from scratch, a golden piece of advice is to begin with the end in mind. As I built my business, I always thought about what would be needed if I was a large Fortune 500 company. While it may take you years to get your second employee (you're the first!), there's no reason why you can't have an operations manual when it's just you. The first year or two, write down the steps you take to complete a task. This will become your manual.

Building a supportive team and having written processes will help when you're thrown curve balls in life. These don't even have to be negative experiences per se. Maternity and paternity leave are a wonderful thing that can take you away from your day-to-day duties. How will your staff know how to maintain your business when you're not right over their shoulder?

4. My Industry Friend

What's true for every industry is that people outside of it can't really understand what it takes to be successful within it. In the wedding industry, we sell stress-free perfection. During consultations, I informed my couples that the only thing I could guarantee is that I would ease the stress that comes with having to make so many decisions in a short period of time. I could not do anything about the stress brought on by overbearing mothers or jealous bridesmaids. As a result, I constantly found myself hiding my true emotions for the sake of keeping my customers delighted.

Once during my separation, I was at a cake consultation. The couple was having a serious and almost heated debate about which flavors to serve during the reception. I distinctly remember thinking, "They're not going to make it. They have *no* idea what lies ahead. If they can't decide between almond and lemon, good luck with deciding on where to spend holidays."

The ability to be able to share this thought and many, many, many more like it with a close industry friend who wouldn't judge me was a relief. My pride didn't allow me to become one of those bitter divorcees who bashed their soon-to-be ex for sympathy.

With that being said, **Be careful who you tell your business to.** This person was not an associate or new friend. We started our businesses at the same time and were supportive throughout the journey. We'd had many personal conversations prior to me sharing my marital troubles. There was a safe and proven track record that this person would keep my confidence. I was very fortunate to have this.

5. My Therapist

Although I talked to myself (yes, myself!), friends and peers, there was one thing I knew for sure—all of these people love me and were not completely impartial. I can also honestly admit that I didn't always tell them the whole story. If my marriage ending up healing, I didn't want them to harbor resentment towards my then husband. So, I sought therapy.

I knew I had to be honest about everything with my therapist if I really wanted a chance at saving my marriage. And let me tell you, there's nothing like having a stranger tell you about yourself. While I didn't get the desired result of staying married, I learned a lot about myself during these sessions. For one, I have a superhero complex and I am a 'fixer'. Project management + wedding planning makes sense now, right?

It's astonishing to me that in this day and age there is still a huge stigma around seeking professional counseling. I would implore any entrepreneur to budget time for this. Therapy comes in many forms: personal 1-on-1 sessions, industry support groups, church seminars and mentorships to name a few. But bear this in mind, if it's not a safe space where you can freely share without fear of judgment, keep it moving until you find such a space.

2020: I'll end with this. In business, it's not being fake to wear the mask when the intentions are good. It's an amazing act of self-lessness towards your clients. Hang in there until you find your fire again!

PS—When you see me smiling at a wedding these days, it's because I've fallen in love with love all over again...

ABOUT SAM

After graduating from East Carolina University's School of Nursing, Samantha Danielle pursued a Master's in Business Administration with a concentration in Healthcare Management. Her goal of becoming a pediatric hospital administrator was deferred once she fell in love with wedding planning. While living in Durham, NC, she opened Bliss By Sam (BBS) Weddings & Occasions in 2005. She then moved herself and the firm to Chicago in 2012.

As a planner, Samantha Danielle recognized the importance of champagne within the wedding industry. The drink itself and the region of Champagne, France became a passion of hers. She decided to close BBS in 2018 and is now pursuing certification as a Master of Champagne through the Wine Scholar Guild.

Samantha Danielle resides in Chicago, IL and her friends say she lives like a tourist. She loves all things Chicago and her favorite places are Soho House and Millennium Park. She also enjoys attending church, cheering for the Dallas Cowboys and traveling internationally.

FAITH, FAILURE, SUCCESS

by Olivia DeMoss

THE RIGHT TO BE AMONG THEM

As I sit in the audience at this seminar filled with highly successful business owners, all—or so it seems—earning multiple six and seven figures, I feel like a fraud. Do I really have the ethical right to be among them? Am I one of them or am I just wishing I were? Am I delusional?

As I beat myself up in silence, I eavesdrop on the conversation the two guys next to me are having:

"I used to have intense anxiety attacks when I was among a group and I was unable to speak up. I am a lot better now, but I still feel like I don't belong when I am in a crowd like this one. I don't measure up to them"

"Would you believe that you are no exception, and that a good percentage of those who are here are also feeling like a fraud?"

What? Thank you! I needed to hear that at this very moment. Though I had heard it multiple times before, and I know that it is a common feeling among coaches, consultants and professionals who guide others on the road to personal or professional success, that imposter syndrome still creeps up occasionally. This nagging monkey on our shoulder whispering in our ear, *How can you help others if you don't fully embody what others see in you?*

» I am not the only one feeling overwhelmed with the pressure to perform up the spiral of self-improvement higher and higher always, in order to offer value to my clients.

» I am not the only one whose mind chatter delivers comparison and self-criticism.

» I am not the only one feeling sometimes that I have no support team other than me and myself.

» I am not the only one with nagging guilt for not yet being the success I feel that I ought to be.

» I am not the only one driven by the constant need to learn more about my subject of expertise and the incessant questioning of, Do I dare call myself an expert?

» I am not the only one battling with non-supportive thoughts and feelings leading to procrastination, fatigue, lack of enthusiasm to start my day, and lack of alignment with my joy—definitely not in the flow of inspiration and creativity.

ME, THE JOY COACH LOSING MY JOY?

Yes, I confess, I am not in a state of joy-filled success all the time. I am human after all! Though at times I feel like superwoman, I have my ups and downs like everyone else. Where I am different is that I don't wallow in non-supportive states of comparison, despair or lack of faith in myself, in the Universe or in my mission. I know how to tap into my joy on demand. Despite my moments of doubt, I know that I am here—I mean, on this planet, in this country that is not my country of birth, and in business—for a special mission. Not just me, but you too, and each one of us is here for a reason and with a gift for the world.

I recently learned a new word: I am a multipotentialite. **Multipotentialites** generally have diverse interests across numerous domains and may be capable of success in many endeavors or professions. They are confronted with unique decisions as a result of these choices. Yes, I am. I have eclectic interests and many talents. I have been successful in various endeavors, and people often tell me that my energy is uplifting, that they appreciate my wisdom and my no-nonsense support. They also tell me that my joy is contagious, so let me contaminate you!

Here are four pillars I encourage you to rely on, as I do:

1. My Business Ethos and My WHY

Is Your Business ethos Crystal Clear to you and to your prospective clients? You are your business. When people buy your services, they buy you; they are attracted by your values. I understand ethos as character, ideology, principles, attitude, the spirit and code of my business, the essence of my WHY—The driving force behind what I do—and the underlying philosophy of my ethics and services, as well as the importance of maintaining high standards of business integrity, along with integrity with myself.

My core values are:

» Always be learning in order to improve myself and add value to my teaching.

» Authenticity and integrity with myself.

» My word is worth a signature.

» My attitude is open, curious, supportive.

» My religion is Nature and my church is the forest.

» I see beauty everywhere; it recharges my batteries and it is available for free.

» I naturally interact with high energy because I am high on Life.

My moto is, Life is a magical adventure that is meant to be enjoyed, and if your life isn't about the joy of it, something needs to change.

— Olivia DeMoss

The WHY behind what I do is my love for Gaia, our gorgeous Planet; and I believe that more joy in people's hearts will lead us closer to peace on Earth.

Answer these questions for yourself:

» What needs am I in business to fulfill?

» Is what I have to offer beneficial to a few or to many?

» Will what I have to offer make a positive difference in the world through the people who work with me? In other words, what is the potential ripple effect?

» Do I have the greater good in mind with my products and services?

» How will society and even the Planet benefit from what I offer?

» Do I know my core values? Are they in the forefront of my decision-making process? Am I willing to compromise them or not?

2. Being Fearless and Taking Action

I was a glass artist for 33 years. Then I became a life coach with many certifications. So, I have always been an entrepreneur: I had to, because I am a rebel and I would absolutely lose my joy if I had to commute to a job every day and punch in every morning; it would suck the life out of me. I am not sure if I chose entrepreneurship or if it chose me, but I celebrate the entrepreneurial spirit every day. Entrepreneurship is the best self-development tool.

Through being an entrepreneur, I came to understand that I

love teaching and transmitting my wisdom and my knowledge which surprised me at first because I didn't like school as a kid. I also helped me appreciate people. When I was a teenager, I used to say, the more I know people the more I like animals...And now love you beautiful people!

I also used to be extremely shy and aware of my accent. So in order to become fearless, I reminded myself that the word "courage" comes from the French "coeur" which means heart. The mission of a coach is to guide people on their journey. Would you agree that coaches have heart? Therefore, in order to be fearless you have to remind yourself that it's not about you. And this actually applies to any industry, not just coaching, because we are all inter-connected. There is no such thing as an independent self. Think about it, all living beings depend on others for their sustenance and well-being. Knowing that I matter and that what I do matters—though I may feel alone at times—I know that I am part of the web of life and that I contribute to the evolution of the human race. This helps me be bold and courageous, it helps me renew my commitment to my mission and it inspires me to keep taking action because it is obvious that having a vision is not enough. If you want something, you have to do something about it. Now, it is not always clear which action to take at which point, and that's why coaching was invented. All successful people have coaches. A coach will lend you an ear, will guide you objectively and support you without judging you. I am a coach and I have several coaches for different aspects of my business.

3. Accountability, Flexibility and Stress

What does success mean to you? Not what others expect of you or what you think it ought to be; what is your idea of success? Be clear about your vision, act upon it every day and take responsibility for your thoughts, actions and results.

We all know that the only constant in life and business is change; and resistance to change only causes stress. Therefore, it makes sense that those who are most adept at navigating change will be the most successful. Being willing and able to adapt to new technology and customers' expectations, new trends—and even foresee situations where adaptability will be required—is a precious asset which is accomplished by openness, creative ways of looking at change, paying attention to your intuition and active listening when in conversation with others.

And of course, the ability to handle stress with grace is of utmost importance because, when you can control stress, it can no longer control you.

—Olivia DeMoss

You see, one of the big problems in the world, and in business today, is that 95% of doctors' visits are related to stress. Stress negatively impacts health, relationships, happiness, productivity and of course, the bottom line. Let me give you some bad news. Time is never going to slow down for professionals like us; in fact, technology will continue to increase our stress. 80% of adults in the US say that they feel stress or anxiety daily, leading to a sixteen-billion-dollar anti-depressant market. Read this part again. Are you contributing to these statistics?

So, what contributes to stress? Here is the answer to remember if you don't want to experience burnout: Stress happens when the demand is higher than the available resources.

How to deal with stress?

» Set boundaries, avoid taking on more than you can reasonably handle, and learn to say NO.

» Be mindful of the company you keep (see next paragraph).

» Practice self-care. Be conscious of what you feed your body and your mind.

» Pay attention to your nutrition, hydration, sleep, and exercise. Read inspirational books, spend time with friends, take on a hobby, adopt a pet. Smile, laugh and play. As a certified therapeutic laughter practitioner, I have studied the benefits of laughter and of course—But of course —I encourage you to hang around people who laugh a lot. Playing and laughing floods your body with feel good hormones that boost your immune system. This also has the power to show you what is most important in life because... when the end comes and you are lying on your death bed, will you regret not having spent more time in the office or will you regret the missed opportunities for laughter?

» Practice daily gratitude, it will change your brain chemistry for the better.

» Recharge your physical, mental, emotional and spiritual batteries by spending time in nature. *In every walk with nature one receives far more than one seeks* —John Muir

» And smile!!! Smiling makes life a whole lot more enjoyable, it is free, it is contagious, and you never know the ripple effects a smile can have. Touching someone with your smile truly is magical, and you just never know how your smile could positively impact someone's life.

4. Environment, Relationships and Overcoming Objections

Human beings are very sensitive to their environment. There is no doubt that you impact your environment, and it also impacts you. Your environment is comprised of your office and your home, the décor and all that you experience through your physical senses, and also the people you interact with.

As far as the places where you live and work:

» The way the furniture is arranged, is it practical? Is it perhaps aligned with Feng Shui principles and set for maximum flow of movement and energy?

» Do you have art or inspirational quotes displayed on the walls or on shelves?

» Are there plants on your desk or on the floor? Plants greatly contribute to cleaning the air, destroying chemical fumes from furniture and carpeting, and also electromagnetic frequencies that are harmful to the cells in your body. Plants also have a soothing effect on the brain.

» Is the room where you work painted in colors that are conducive to creativity and well being?

» Is your space cluttered or harmoniously organized?

All of these have an impact on your well-being and your productivity. Your choice of physical environment—and this includes the way you dress—is a mirror of your inner environment. When your space is disharmonious, it is hard to feel good, inspired and productive.

The same thing goes for the company you keep. It is said that you are a reflection of the five people closest to you. Do they believe in you and support you or are you surrounded by nay-sayers and jealous people? Are they successful, energetic, positive and happy or do they have a victim mentality? Have a circle of friends who believe in you. Often our family members are not our supporters because they knew us before we were successful, and it is very hard to change initial perceptions.

As for overcoming objections, I am sure you have heard that people do business with those they know, like and trust; it is all about trust and likeability. I have a soft approach to objections. I say: before anything else, you have to be true to yourself. Love and respect yourself enough to be in touch with your values and honor them. If I offer you a service that I know will benefit you, I want you to measure the cost of not investing in yourself. How much is it going to cost you professionally, in your relationships, your health, your well-being and your joy—or lack thereof?

Here are a few more things I have learnt from being in business for myself:

» My time is valuable; It is my most precious asset. Over the last few years, I have learnt to respect and honor it, and I ferociously protect it. I say NO without feeling bad about it. I encourage you to prioritize your professional and your private life in a way that is aligned with your values.

» Moments of doubt and fear are inevitable, but deep down, you have to believe in yourself and have faith in the perfect order of things—even when it doesn't make sense to you. Trust your intuition, it knows better than your rational mind.

» Give yourself permission to quit. Sometimes it is by quitting that a better opportunity shows up. I am not advocating quitting on a whim, but you have to distinguish between being stubborn and being persistent. Have a vision that pulls you forward.

» See failure, not as a defeat but as a valuable learning experience. It wasn't a failure; you just got off track for a while. Reconnect to your vision, stay curious and open to opportunities that may be foreign to your habitual set up. Have a can do, positive attitude.

» Don't believe everything you think. Your reptilian (or primal) brain is not the part of the brain that encourages you to be bold. Its role is to keep you safe; therefore, it sees anything unfamiliar as a potential threat and can greatly hinder your ability to think rationally. To that extent, it generates mind chatter, creating self-doubt, fear and all kinds of non-supportive and even toxic emotions that keep you safe, thus, preventing you from taking risks and reaching your utmost potential. These non-supportive thoughts and beliefs might come from the voices of people who discouraged, criticized or ridiculed you some time ago, or from past experiences even as far back as early childhood. Can you gather the courage to question these beliefs? Are they trying to tell you something about you? Perhaps something about your behavior that results in these emotions? Will you dare listen to them and put them to the test? Is it time to adopt a change from within and to take responsibility for your inner as well as your outer life?

» Do not indulge in self-criticism. Instead, get into the habit of feeding your mind positive thoughts and beauty to raise your vibration, listening to inspirational speakers and spending time in Nature.

» Connect your head with your heart. Somebody said that these twelve inches are the longest journey you'll ever take, and it is true. Science has discovered that your heart knows things before your head does. The Institute of HeartMath and other organizations as well, have demonstrated that the heart has its own brain that constantly communicates with the brain in your head. When the heart and the brain are in coherence, you experience greater clarity and ease in decision making, clearer intuitive hints and flow. When you feel positive emotions like caring, appreciation, compassion, love and gratitude, the heart's rhythm becomes more coherent. This also sends endorphins and oxytocin throughout your body, giving you a high and boosting your energy and resilience.

» Put systems in place. When do recurring tasks need get done– daily, weekly, monthly? For example, changing your water filter every six months. Put those tasks on your calendar and they won't be burdening your brain any longer.

» Learn to ask for help. It is not a weakness, and in fact, people usually like to help, it makes them feel valued.

I trust that you found these tips valuable, I wish you the best of success in your endeavors, along with lots of joy, and...Remember to keep smiling!

ABOUT OLIVIA

Life has brought Olivia into contact with a variety of cultures, experiences and challenges on different continents. Though she was born in Paris, France, she is a citizen of the World. She has a reverence for Life; she is an advocate for animals, the environment and our gorgeous Planet; and she loves gardening and being in Nature.

A life-long glass artist turned coach, author and speaker with a calling to help push humanity forward, she helps her audience understand that a major source of discontentment comes from compromising our own truth. Olivia believes that more "Joie de vivre" (joy of living) in people's hearts will lead us closer to peace on Earth. Her motto is, "Life is a magical adventure that is meant to be enjoyed, and if your Life isn't about the joy of it, something needs to change!"

Reach out to Olivia at:
Olivia@JoyAndAbundanceByDesign.com
www.JoyAndAbundanceByDesign.com
https://www.facebook.com/olivia.demoss
https://www.linkedin.com/in/oliviademoss/

MORE ON FAITH

Faith is standing up every time you fall because your belief in Him calls you to that commitment.

— Jennifer Christenson

Faith, according to Scripture, is the substance of things hoped for, the evidence of things not seen. It's your beliefs. Faith is necessary to connect us with the spiritual being of God, and it makes Him become real to us. Having faith is necessary to grow and be successful in every aspect of our lives. The spiritual aspect of our lives is to be fed with the knowledge and understanding of our Father so that our relationship with Him grows strong. It is necessary to have a strong bond with Him in order to listen to his guidance and recognize the path you are on. In the business world, faith in God and faith in yourself is vital. It's about getting to know yourself as well. You need to be self-confident in the direction you're moving and in the decisions you are making. Faith is the belief in yourself and it is your belief in God. If your faith is strong, it can take away your worries, stresses, and fears and give you confidence in the work you are doing. Faith was my main weapon in my fight against stage 4 cancer. It is very powerful and under used in this world. Faith should be ever-growing as we learn about ourselves while we experience life.

—Mary Stowers, Cancer Survivor

What you make happen for others, God will make happen for you! To me, faith means to act on what I believe. It is very important and vital to develop and grow your faith. That is a daily activity and achieved through reading and listening to things that build up your faith and mindset. If there is something that I have a desire for, it starts with hope. Then, I visualize it before I have it, and that's where my faith starts to kick into action. With faith, you have to see it before you actually see it. There are times in your life, whether it is something small or something significant, when you desire to do or have but are unsure how it will happen. That is when your faith will have to be utilized. Regardless of how long it may take to acquire what you are desiring, you still have to see yourself with whatever it is you want. Yes, there will be opposition, distractions and numerous things that tell you that you can't do it or have it, but when you have developed your faith walk, nothing can stop you from getting what you truly desire! First see it before you see it; write your goals or plans for it; conquer it! Just as importantly, speak positively over what you are believing to happen! Your words are very powerful when you are using your faith to accomplish and acquire what you want!

— Johnnita Robinson, Entrepreneur

As a businesswoman or not, faith is the most integral part of who I am. My faith is something I can neither escape...nor live without. It is my anchor, guidepost and safest point of security. In business it is the voice reminding me that serving others well is my mission and that God is my provider, not people or even my own arduous effort. It is also the voice that reminds me that self-care and a good rhythm to my life matters. In business I work hard and faithfully but also to create a rhythm of rest.

My faith also allows me to believe that it is God's heart for me to be blessed through my work. That it is His intent that I should find joy in my work. I love the scripture in Ecclesiastes 5:18-20 that says, "It is good and fitting for one to eat and drink and to enjoy the good of all his labor in which he toils under the sun all the days of his life which God gives him; for it is his heritage. As for every man to whom God has given riches and wealth and given him power to eat of it. To receive his heritage and rejoice in his labor—this is the gift of God. For he will not dwell unduly on the days of his life because God keeps him busy with the joy of his heart."

In my mind faith and integrity are interrelated. It is my faith that inspires me to walk honestly and with integrity in business, knowing that God's blessing will undergird my integrity. He will back me up through errors, mistakes and flaws. My part is to always operate, seen and unseen, in ways that are filled with integrity.

— Christine E. Burlison

For me, faith has always been attached to a belief in the "unknown", a higher power. Evidence of the "unseen". It means constantly putting my trust into something bigger than me. As the late Rev. Dr. Johnnie Colemon stated, "It works if you work it". When all hope seems to be gone, it is not my job to understand the who, what, when, where, why and how but to stand firm in knowing that I will prevail without a shadow of doubt. To help strengthen my conviction, I constantly utilize spiritual tools as well as revisit personal testimonies.

—Shari C. Hill , MBA, MHRM

Faith is belief that we are all one with a higher source and that higher power is always looking out for us. It always wants the very best for us, and all involved, no matter what things may look like in the natural.

—Tangee Moscoso

F = Forgetting

A = All

I = Instead

T = Trusting

H = Him

That means believing in YOUR PURPOSE when no one else see it. FAITH sees what you don't see it, yet you BELIEVE it. This is why I keep going, because of my FAITH!!!

—Cortez Mack

Faith fuels my ambition; it allows me to think big, guides my decisions, moves my feet, and brings about wins.

—Alisa Inez

Life is a journey full of twists and turns and faith is your guide through it.

—Connie Glover

My Thank You letter to FAITH.

Thank you Faith, for introducing yourself to me very early in my life. My childhood traumas made me search for you. I knew there was a purpose for my life, and I knew that I wanted bigger and more for myself. Statistically, growing up on the Westside of Chicago, my chances were not that great. Society said that I should be comfortable with lack of education, "affordable housing" and a job, not a career. But, thanks to you Faith, I knew that I needed an education. I knew that I needed more, so I worked hard on my craft and on myself. I made some huge mistakes along with the way, but the way that my FAITH was set up, I knew that I had to just keep praying and keep moving by any means necessary. I couldn't see you, but since I was a little girl, I've always known that you were right by my side. As I continue on my path, something tells me that everything I encounter will be handled with greatness. I'm excited about my future. Thank you Faith...

—Keisha Rose, Co-CEO

G-Rose Productions,

Actress, Model, Writer

Faith, to me, is truly believing that God has an amazing plan for me and when He gives me opportunities to better myself, I need to believe and trust His plan!!

—Tammy Lyn Connors

I have discovered in my life that most people have faith in faith or in an institution, but not in God. My faith is in the One who controls the seas, heals disease, and casts out demons. I have seen Him work in my life and it builds my faith in Him every time. Putting faith in anything or anyone else is futile!

—Dee Stokes

Your success and failures are measured by your faith in God and yourself. Faith is believing a power outside of yourself will reveal the power within to make your dreams a reality. It's the foundation or platform that helps direct my decisions while learning to trust the process. I think it's simple—faith and trust must go hand in hand. Faith is having spiritual values and good character operating in alignment for the better good.

—Robert Hazzard

Faith to me, is believing in the "impossible". Believing in what can't be seen, granted by the grace of God. Having faith as small as a mustard seed produces large blessings received from just believing in what God can give and provide me.

—Mona McIlwain

Faith is about realizing you can't do anything of value all by your-self—it's not all about you—it's all about being part of something bigger than you. That means putting your trust in God, and in the people God brings into your life. You have to have faith in yourself, of course, but at the end of the day, the wise person knows when to graciously accept advice and help. Sometimes it's a temptation to put all your faith in yourself, when what you really need is to have some faith in others. And when things don't go your way, and there is suffering, faith is the conviction to continue to believe in God and in goodness, recognizing that you are not the center of the universe.

—James L. Papandrea, M.Div., Ph.D.

Faith means believing our circumstances can always get better. There are times in life in which we're faced with situations that appear to be insurmountable. We worry about the outcome, not knowing what's waiting for us down the road. We may go to bed with fears, but faith is knowing we can wake up with a renewed sense of energy and hope. Faith is believing the gift of today will be better than the challenges of yesterday.

—Anthony Ellis McGee

Under faith lies strength. When you think of the word "faith", you think more so of patience and the willingness to await the outcome of what you are praying about as well as your concerns. I also see faith as a source of strength. In personal or business, I have to have the courage and belief that whatever decision I make or blueprint I create requires applying strength to my faith to hold fast and stand still to see it through. Having faith can be hard a lot of times but it is such a relief when the outcome is positive because you were strong enough to hold on to your faith.

—Toni Nicole

Without faith, guidance from the Father and confidence in yourself, it would be difficult to lead, not only yourself, but others to success. As they say, faith nourishes the heart and soul.

—Mary Stowers, Cancer Survivor

FAILURE

Understanding the concept of what failure truly means has taken some time because I was taught to be a perfectionist very early in my life. Being raised in the church, I was constantly living up to a standard that was unattainable, if I were to grow. There was no room for mistakes. Any misstep I made was cause for depression and self-flagellation because I "should have known better." Only with therapy, reading a lot of helpful spiritual texts, and continuous prayer and meditation did I start to give myself a break. I truly believe that there is no such thing as failure. There is only maturation, no matter how painful. Every "failure" has taken me to a new level on my journey in life.

—Cynda Williams

FAILURE IS THE FERTILIZER OF SUCCESS

by Mel Roberson

S how me a man or a woman who has never failed, and I will show you a man or woman who has never tried. In the society that we live in, people are afraid to fail. It's understandable why. You don't want to be laughed at, mocked, embarrassed, or hurt. I believe that it is my duty to inform you that the fear of failure is learned. It's not real! At some point in your life you developed a fear of failure because of something somebody said to you. Or maybe it was an experience that happened where you were teased as a child. The reality is that mankind has only succeeded because of failure. It is the fertilizer for success. Not in the smelly way you may think of fertilizer, but in a way that aids in yielding maximum results.

Let's journey back to when you were a toddler. I know this may be hard for you to remember but try to think back to when you first learned to walk. If you cannot remember that far back, think about a child you witnessed learning to walk. This was a grand adventure! You would pull yourself up by using the couch or coffee table... Wobbly legs and all...You would venture for a few steps in then... BOOM! You fell flat on your bottom! What happened next? Was it the end of the world? Did it lower your self-esteem? Did you give up and declare, "This walking thing just isn't for me! I will crawl for the rest of my life!" Could you imagine if there were a group of people who gave up attempting to walk before they were even a year old and would have to be carried by family members for the rest of their lives? That would be utterly ridiculous. Funny, but utterly ridiculous.

Most toddlers are fearless! Somehow though, we lose that courageous spirit as we mature. It could be for a variety of reasons however, none of those reasons are good enough to steal your fire. What fire you ask? The fire that is divine and burns in each and every one of us. It is our responsibility to do something great in the world. The challenge is that the world often beats us up and makes us afraid to fail. It is not winning that makes us better, it is actually failing. Napoleon Hill, the author of the world-renowned book, *Think and Grow Rich*, says that every adversity carries with it a seed of equivalent or greater benefit. This includes every failure you have ever experienced. Failure is only failure if you don't learn from it. We need the failures to make us grow. We need to figure out the ways to do it wrong first, so that we can do it right forever. Many people clean their homes with a cleaning solution called Formula 409. It works great! The story behind the story is that the cleaning solution received that name after two scientists from Detroit failed 408 times before getting a batch that actually worked the way they wanted it to. That's right! Formula 409 received its name because of the 408 failures before it!

In my 20 years of being an entrepreneur, I have learned to embrace failure. I don't plan on failing, but when it happens, I embrace it. I look for the lessons that I can receive from the experience. I look for the growth that will come because of it. I look for signs and clues of why I failed so that I don't make the same mistakes again. Failure has become my friend. We have a strange relationship, but I love it. Again, we learn more from losing than we do from winning. It's great to have an expectation for success! It is also great to have a positive mental attitude to get you through the failures! Both are necessary to be successful in life and business.

One of my careers is as an actor. I've been on several major net work television shows, films, and stage plays. I have had far more auditions than the number of projects I've actually been in. Every "no" got me closer to a "yes". Every failure gave me an opportunity to evaluate my skills and see how I could return better than I was the last time. If I gave up after my first few auditions when I didn't get booked for a show, I would have never ended up on Chicago P.D. (NBC), Empire (Fox), or The Chi (Showtime Network) to name a few. You may not hit every shot, but I will guarantee you that you will miss 100% of the shots that you do not take.

One of the major reasons that people give up is because they continuously compare themselves to someone else. This is a huge mistake. Your primary competition is with your previous best self. People have different learning curves. The path to success is not the same for everyone. Though it may be similar, your experience will be unique for you. Your failures may be somewhat unique for you. Depending on your industry, you may be able to find a mentor that can help you avoid some of the pitfalls. Ultimately though, you will make mistakes. There is nothing wrong with that. Embrace them. Learn to love them because you learn from them.

If you have ever been on an airplane, or seen one takeoff, there is something amazing that has to happen in order for the aircraft to achieve lift. It needs negative wind resistance. What I mean by that is the aircraft needs to go against the wind—Fight the wind—in order for it to take off. There has to be enough wind under the wings for it to achieve lift, so it races at a fast pace cutting into the wind in order to reach its ultimate goal of takeoff. Human beings want to achieve lift or take off without the negativity. In all actuality, the adversity that we go through on our way to our goals improves the prize at the end of the race. The journey towards success is not about the end result. It is about what you become on your way to the end result. If you become somebody worthy of millions of dollars, it doesn't matter if those millions of dollars get lost in a bad investment. They could even be stolen from you. The thing that is the most important is who you became in the process of earning those millions of dollars. The person that you became in order to earn that type of income is the person that you know how to be... Not once, not twice, but you are that person. This is why millionaires and billionaires who have lost it all before can get it right back. This is why athletes who get injured can recover and get back on the field. This is why anybody who is at the top of their game is able to experience a setback and get back to where they were before. It's really about mindset. It's really about embracing the failures that you've gone through, learning from them, and propelling yourself into the future towards the goal or desire that you ultimately want.

I don't want you to think that I assume this is easy for people to understand and practice. I completely understand how it could be difficult to shift your mindset to one of success through embracing failure if you've had all of these different experiences all of your life telling you otherwise. What I do want you to think about is when you first became consciously aware that you were afraid to fail. What was the incident that took place that scared you? What was the event that made you feel like it was easier for you to set small goals and achieve them than it was for you to achieve large goals and conquer them? What did somebody say to you that made you believe that you were not a giant? It was at that moment that you decided that it was easier to play it safe than it was to go after what your heart really desired. Most human beings are still making decisions as a five or seven-year-old. You need to identify that defining moment when you accepted that you were less than amazing. That is where you may be basing your decisions from. You could be 40 years old still making decisions as a seven-year-old. You held on to that experience and no longer gave yourself permission to be great.

In some cases, there was no outside force that made you want to play small. Some of us can be our own worst enemies. In those cases, we are the ones that told ourselves we are not good enough, we are not smart enough, and we should not try hard to become something better than what we currently are. At some point, you have to decide if you really want what you desire. Success happens when your work ethic meets your desires. You have to do the work! And you have to not be afraid of failure. Instead of you being that 5 to 7-year-old who is afraid of failure, go back to that 10-month-old that doesn't know the difference. Go back to the time when you were willing to try anything. That's where your power lies.

I once heard a story that took place in Minnesota. It was about three little boys who lived in a community near a lake. That could be anywhere because they called Minnesota the land of 10,000 lakes. At any rate, the three little boys were best friends who spent the majority of their free time together. On Sunday afternoons after church, they would keep their dress shoes on and go sliding around on one of the lakes as if they were ice-skating. One of the little boys went too far out and fell through the ice. He floated under the ice and was trapped. He was drowning! Another little boy ran back to town to get help. The little boy that was under the ice was being raised by his grandmother because his parents were deceased. The third little boy that stayed behind to keep an eye on his friend followed him under the ice. Watching one of his best friends die...Slowly—It was agonizing. Off in the distance, he saw a huge tree trunk and decided to take action. He ran and lifted the tree trunk, carried it to where his friend was, broke the ice and pulled his friend to safety! The people from town got there shortly after and were amazed at what they saw. The fire chief came and asked the third little boy who had pulled his friend to safety, "What happened?"

The boy replied, "I didn't want my friend to die, so I grabbed that tree trunk to break the ice. Then I pulled him out."

The fire chief said, "You're too small...no really, please tell me what happened."

The boy said again (this time somewhat doubting himself), "I...uh...didn't want my...uh... friend to die, so I...uh... grabbed that tree trunk and broke the ice..."

Now the fire chief was getting upset! He asked one more time, in an extremely stern voice, "I need you to *honestly* tell me what happened!"

The scared little boy started to tell him what happened again, and before he could complete his first sentence the grandmother of the other little boy who almost drowned jumped in and said, "I'll tell you what happened! *You* weren't here to tell him that he *couldn't* do it!"

How many times has that happened in life? How many times have you been afraid to try something great because someone else told you that you would fail? Just because someone told you that you can't do something doesn't mean that it's true! You can do anything that you set your mind to and are willing to work for. It's up to you. Yes—you may fail a couple of times along the way, but if you don't give up, SUCCESS will be yours! My good friend Harold Branch III once said, "The harder I fall, the higher I bounce." That is one of the rules I live by now. Do not be afraid to fail. It's going to happen. What happens after the failure is the important part. I think that you are an incredible human being! The fact that you are taking time to read this means that you want more for yourself. I have one request for you. Do me a huge favor, please.

GO BE AMAZING!

ABOUT MEL

Mel Roberson is a four-time Amazon best-selling author. On three projects, he was a contributing author. His first solo project, *31 Amazing Life Lessons of Joshua Stokes*, hit the Amazon best-seller rankings in several different categories.

Mel is a Chicago native, and delivers professional development seminars for corporations and organizations across North America. He was a victim of gun violence at age 17 and believes that his life was spared so that he could be an example for others. He has spoken in front of crowds as large as 15,000 people. He currently serves as the Network Vice President of Illinois and Wisconsin for the company, LegalShield. In the evening, he is an accomplished actor and an award-winning poet/spoken word artist. He's been on shows such as Chicago P.D. (NBC), Empire (FOX), and The Chi (Showtime). He believes that his most important job on earth is as a father to his beautiful daughters.

Reach out to Mel:
Instagram: @TheTotalGent
Website: www.MelRoberson.com
Youtube: Melevation

FIND A WAY

by Glenn Murray

As a publisher, it goes without saying that I read a lot. I have consumed countless articles, books, stories, manuscripts, and blogs. The works I seem to find most compelling are those stories of people who have overcome near impossible odds to accomplish great things. It's not just about a person being the underdog. What is inspiring to me is the profile that is developed once they've been through the fire. I've never been big on excuses, I make few. I believe when you have a goal, a dream, a desire, a passion, a small voice inside (whatever you call your inspiring spirit)—there is nothing that can stop you. As a sports fan, I appreciate the drive of athletes and the talent and focus they must possess to be at the top of their game. I especially love the stories of those who achieve while not necessarily meeting the perceived "requirements" of a sport that guarantee success. Case in point, Doug Flutie. Flutie played quarterback at a time when every college recruiter and professional scout thought quarterbacks should be at least six feet tall. Flutie was five foot-ten, and that may have been a generous measurement. He looked, at times, like a high schooler playing with the big kids. Only one Division I school, Boston College, recruited him. In my opinion and given the jersey number he was assigned (22), they thought he would end up being a receiver or defensive back, never a quarterback.

By his senior year, he had amassed more passing yards than any college quarterback who had previously played. He won the Heisman Trophy, college football's equivalent to an MVP award, and his "Hail Mary" last-second, touchdown pass to beat the defending National Champion Miami Hurricanes in 1983 was so famous, according to an article in Boston College Magazine, the number of students applying for admission to the school increased! Flutie not only was an outstanding athlete; he was an outstanding student. He was also a finalist for the prestigious Rhodes scholarship.

Despite what 200 other coaches, scouts, and experts said could never happen, Doug Flutie found a way. He was able, despite all the perceived limitations (height being the most obvious), to make his talent shine, and he didn't stop there! As he moved into the professional ranks, the size expectations to play quarterback in the NFL were even more heavily scrutinized. In the NFL Network documentary, A Football Life, Flutie addressed these concerns head on. "Can a guy who's five-foot-nine, 175 pounds make it in the pros?", he answered "Yes, he can. But it's a matter of ability and not size. I feel I can play; I don't know for sure, and those questions will be answered in the future." After bouncing around to a couple of teams in the USFL and NFL, Flutie found his niche in the Canadian Football League (CFL). The pace was faster and the style of play more wide open. It was a perfect match for his skill set. In eight years in the CFL, Flutie became one of that league's greatest players winning three league championships. He returned to the NFL and led the Buffalo Bills to the playoffs (only to be benched for the playoff game for the returning starting quarterback. In my opinion, this was one of the dumbest coaching moves ever. It's no wonder Buffalo has zero Super Bowl wins!). Flutie would end up as the oldest player at the time to score a touchdown in league history, the oldest to play quarterback in a game and even scored an extra point with a drop kick during his final season with the New England Patriots. His ability and will to keep playing despite the perception of many experts shows that it really is the ability you display and the belief in yourself that keeps you finding a way to succeed.

As I was doing research for this chapter, I thought about the many examples I could write about. Sports was my default but there was another example that was just so remarkable, I actually didn't believe it when I first read it. The story of French author Jean-Dominique Bauby is one that is as amazing as it is unique. Bauby was editor of the popular French version of the fashion magazine, Elle. In 1995, at the age of 43, he had a cerebrovascular seizure that left him unconscious for 20 days. When he awoke, he was completely paralyzed. His brain had been severed from his spinal cord; and he could not breathe, swallow or eat without assistance— save his ability to blink his left eye. Not able to speak, move or care for himself, he was attended to by his wife, his son, and his daughter. He was suffering from "Locked in Syndrome", a condition in which the victim is aware but cannot move or communicate due to complete paralysis of nearly all voluntary muscles in his or her body except for eye movements and blinking. The individual is conscious and cognitively able to communicate with eye movements. With this reality in the prime of what was an exciting and eventful life, Bauby often lamented each moment as he was trapped with his thoughts to truly analyze. In an interview, he communicated to writer Thomas Mallon, "One day...I can find it amusing, in my 45th year, to be cleaned up and turned over, to have my bottom wiped and swaddled like a newborn's. I even derive a guilty pleasure from this total lapse into infancy. But the next day, the same procedure seems to me unbearably sad, and a tear rolls down through the lather a nurse's aide spreads over my cheeks." Through this unimaginable bout of adversity at the height of his career, Bauby found a way to communicate.

A system called partner-assisted scanning, a communication strategy that allows an individual with physical and/or visual impairments to communicate more actively by participating in conversations using choices presented aloud, provided patients with the language they needed to interact and the ability to cue their communication partner to provide more appropriate choices. It was using this system that Bauby learned to communicate. Once able to "talk" to visitors, he began sending friends what he called "samizdat" bulletins. From these was born the idea of an entire book. Bauby already had a publishing contract so he hired Claude Mendibil, a freelance editor, to work with him. After two months of writing and two weeks of editing, the book was completed. Not only did he communicate, but he also wrote his book, *The Diving Bell and The Butterfly*. Using a rearranged French alphabet based on the most frequently used letters, Bauby wrote and edited the entire book in his head then dictated it one blink at a time. The book is a metaphor for his condition. The diving bell, a deep-sea diver in one of those heavy, old-fashioned diving suits, represented his paralyzed state. The butterfly described the state of his mind, fluttering like a rare butterfly from memory to memory. It took him about 200,000 blinks to write the book of slightly more than 100 pages, Mendibil calculated when asked in a Los Angeles times story. The book was released in 1997, and in its first week sold over 100,000 copies. It became a major motion picture and won awards at the Cannes Film Festival, the Golden Globes, the BAFTAs, and the César Awards. It also received four Academy Award nominations. Several critics listed it as one of the best films of the decade. From extreme adversity to accomplishment, this story is one I like to use when I encounter fully functional people procrastinating about book writing! IF YOU CAN BLINK IT YOU CAN ACHIEVE IT.

Nothing is impossible. Find A Way.

Encouragement through entrepreneurship and through life are key. The examples I used here are great examples of people overcoming adversity. My last example is even closer to me and my most fond remembrance. It's the story of my mother Joyce. She was diagnosed with stage 4 lung cancer and even through that tough period, she continued her job as an online college instructor, continued to work on 2 books and finished her PhD...all while undergoing painful radiation and chemotherapy treatments. I've never seen anyone maximize their 24 hours like she did. She instilled in me the desire to be great every day even though every day wasn't going to be great. Cancer, while it robbed me of being able to have her here to read this as I write about her as my true hero, couldn't delay her goals and dreams; and up to her last day on this earth, she never stopped setting goals. She never stopped telling the people she loved how she felt about them. She never stopped fighting, she never stopped living. She is why this chapter exists. With these stories, I wanted to show you that the physical and the mental can have tremendous effects on our personal environment. But it's the mind, the belief, the desire to find a way that helps us accomplish what sometimes seems impossible. Take a moment and ask yourself, "What's blocking me right now?" I can guarantee you it's not a 250-pound linebacker like Doug Flutie faced, I pray its not a physical ailment like paralysis or cancer.

Maybe it's your environment? Maybe it's the people in your circle? What is your diving bell? Holding you at the bottom of an ocean of doubt, indecision, and failure? What's paralyzing you mentally? What are you waiting for? Many have accomplished much more with less than you have at this very moment. There is nothing worse than a world of talented failures...So I challenge you today, and every day. FIND A WAY

ABOUT GLENN

Glenn Murray is the founder of 220 Communications, the parent company to 220 Publishing and Food Wine and Spirit Ventures. Through 220 Publishing, he has published more than 50 titles across all genres. As a writer, Glenn has blogged for the NBC Chicago Street Teams, contributed articles to *360 Magazine*, authored the blog, "Stop, Look, Listen", for Chicagonow.com and contributed to "The Entrepreneur Within You" book series. In 2019, he released his first solo work, "You Wrote It, Now Go Sell It, A Marketing and Promotions Guide for Authors in A Few Simple Steps".

He co-cofounded the film and television production entity, G-Rose Productions. He's co-written four film scripts, including one based on a 220 Publishing release, "Love Miscarriage", and two television series. He co-produces the un-scripted series, *Making Love Better Twogether* and *Live From the Cave*. He has been featured in *Rolling Out*, Ebony/Jet Online and the *Chicago Sun Times*, *Voyage Atlanta Magazine* and *The Backstory Television Show*. He was selected by *The Chicago Defender* as one of the "50 Men of Excellence" and has been a frequent guest on the *Smart Marketing for Small Business Radio Show*, *The Color of Wine Podcast* and

The Live Exchange Radio Show.

Reach out to Glenn:

220communications.com

MORE ON FAILURE

Because something doesn't work out at the moment...doesn't mean that it's not going to work out at all. That just means it wasn't the right time/season for me to receive it.

—Cortez Mack

You're only a failure if you stay inside the comfort of your cocoon and never find your wings and fly out into the unknown.

—Connie Glover

Failure to me means that I have not succeeded in what I started out to do. It means that I did not do as well as I knew I could have done even if my ultimate goal is accomplished. Failure is not using the many gifts and talents of which we are blessed. When I managed employees I did not feel successful unless they were successful as I was there leader. If one of my employees failed at something it was my failure as well. A good leader has to take ownership and responsibility for his or her team. Otherwise there is failure.

—Mary Stowers, Cancer Survivor

Failing at something doesn't necessarily make me a failure. It just means that I can learn from it and re-attempt to accomplish it. A lot of times people think that because they didn't complete a goal or something didn't go as plan, they are a failure. To me, that is so far from the truth. If anything, never trying to accomplish something, that could contribute to being a failure, because you never put one foot forward to start. But I would never consider someone a failure regardless of what they did or didn't do. Failing forward is the best example of learning from your mistakes. And there will be times when you do. But I truly don't believe that makes you a failure.

—Johnnita Robinson, Entrepreneur

Failure has a myriad of meanings and creates an assortment of actions. Failure has a negative impact on us if we're afraid of it. In order to fail at something, first we have to be willing to take a risk to get the reward we're seeking. If viewed properly, failures are the lessons we learn during the process to reaching our goals. They're building blocks. We should view failure through the eyes of toddlers: No matter how many times babies fall, they're always willing to get up until they're able to walk.

—Anthony Ellis McGee

Failing, to me, is only an eye opener to know that what wasn't achieved just wasn't meant for me. I feel that failure can be viewed as a positive more than a negative. It's more of a learning process for me. What can I do better to achieve what I really want? Maybe God has plans for me to achieve something else?

—Mona McIlwain

There is no such thing as failure, but instead are lessons to cherish because they help guide us to the parts that need healing, redirecting, or new direction. So, love these challenges the most because they bring the most growth.

—Tangee Moscoso

To me, failure means that I did not achieve an intended outcome based on the vision and goals that I anticipated accomplishing at that particular time. This can be in or out of my control. If I feel like omething was a failure, it was a major disappointment for me as I don't see many things I've experienced as failures. Most of the time f something doesn't go well, I simply see it as a life lesson.

—Shari C. Hill , MBA, MHRM

Failure is not trying. Failure is a lack of integrity, hurting others, and refusing the opportunities to use your voice for truth. Failure is believing in fear before faith.

—Jennifer Christenson

Failure to me is a very tough word. Instead of failure, I call it "life-learning lessons". Once I learn the lesson, I can move forward and try things a different way.

—Tammy Lyn Connors

Failure means success—one should not let what has been deemed as non-successful, be the end all and/or fatal. Failure is in the faith of the beholder. Pivoting at the right time or understanding when it's time to change directions is a necessity. Your faith will reveal what others view as a failure, but it can be a steppingstone. The experience itself will strengthen you which is a positive and should not be viewed as a negative. Failures are learning and growing experiences to be used and viewed as success in the making

—Robert Hazzard

Failure is not defined in terms of the obstacles or setbacks we encounter. Every path to success is paved with obstacles and set-backs. On the other hand, sometimes goals need to be reevaluated. So failure cannot even be defined in terms of quitting, or giving up.

Failure is quitting when the right thing to do is keep going. But faiure can also be a stubborn persistence when the right thing to do i to let something go.

—James L. Papandrea, M.Div., Ph.D

SUCCESS

Success is another concept that I've evolved in. Each moment of each day, I succeed. Every step I take in this life takes me to the next evolving stage. I believe I am constantly moving forward, even if the steps I take keep me in a repetitive pattern for a while. I am being taught a lesson that I will use later on. I am always learning. Now, all new knowledge doesn't necessarily feel good, especially if I find out that my convictions were flawed, but it is a successful experience when I learn from it. Success isn't always about the things I am celebrated for. Sometimes the small kernel of expansion I have, truly seeing the picture-perfect sky and knowing that I am abundantly blessed is as important to memorialize. The act of living itself is success.

—Cynda Williams

SUCCESS IN BUSINESS:
EFFECTIVE MARKETING FOR TODAY'S NONPROFITS AND SMALL BUSINESSES

by Leonard Mogul

Our greatest glory consists not in never falling, but in rising every time we fall.

—Oliver Goldsmith

Have you ever wondered why some things gain traction while others fall flat before they have a chance to gain momentum? Today's nonprofits and small business-es are faced with the exponential challenge of setting themselves apart from all others. Establishing credibility is essential for any organization to gain trust in today's highly competitive world. Cer-tainly, this is nothing new, as one readily realizes that before others contribute time and money to your cause or invest in your venture, you must establish a reputation that is beyond reproach.

All sounds good on paper but, "How does one get started?" you may ask. What tools do you employ and how do you garner support beyond your immediate family and friends?" This chapter will show you how to do just that. It will teach you how to utilize your proac-tive "aunt" who you always thought was way too social, how to use certain online resources, how to make an impression with your printed material and finally, how to get media to help carry your message to the masses. All of this and more will be discussed here. Let's get started, shall we?

"SPEAKING IT EASY" - WORD OF MOUTH

An idea has been lingering in your mind for months. You can envision it but, "How do you bring it to life?" Herein is where the challenge lies. You reach out to your "aunt" whom you have always thought was super charged with energy and uncanny social skills. No matter where she went, she made friends and seemed to always attend a variety of social events. You share with her your idea to start your new venture to help a great cause or to establish a small business. I will not name the venture as the basic principles for marketing any particular cause or small business are similar. You convince her to help you carry your message—a good start indeed!

"What's my next step?" lingers in your mind. After all, every move is essential, and a single misstep may cause things to spiral out of control. You begin to ponder whom to reach out to for help with carrying your message. Your organization, in its infancy, must create strategic alliances with proven community leaders who know you. Reaching out to people who are not familiar with you or the body of your work is not necessarily in your best interest. Sharing your idea, before it takes flight, with people who you don't know well may cause someone to try and make your idea their own. Hence, it is best to take essential steps to protect your ideas. Some basic strategies will be discussed later.

For the "word of mouth" strategy to bear fruit, you must find allies and form strategic partnerships. Believing that your message will resonate with all you speak to is a mindless task. People are more likely to identify with your message or concept if it has everyday value (something they can use), and/or it has emotional importance (a thing they can identify with) to them. Furthermore, people are more receptive to a message when it is told as a story and not lectured to them. In other words, your message has to flow, and you should make it pliable to fit the course of the conversation. Thus, before you are ready to deliver your message to the masses, make sure to practice it in front of the mirror, then your sibling, then friends, and only after then, will come others.

"GETTING SOCIAL WITH IT" AND E-MAIL MARKETING CAM-PAIGNS

Social media undoubtedly has its benefits. This is a free resource that we utilize on a daily basis to communicate with the "world" can and should be used to further our cause. However, let's address a few caveats before you jump on your computer and create a group and/or a business page. Unlike sharing your goals with your "aunt," by marketing through any of the social media platforms you reveal your plans to the "world." For starters, in order to protect your interests, it is of utmost importance to safeguard your ideas by ensuring that you register your organization and acquire a domain name.

Choosing between creating a group and a business page can be tricky. Both have their benefits, but what works best for your purpose depends on the time that you are willing to invest. My personal experience has been that both are valuable tools. Both can work together as an effective information delivery system. For instance, a group is easier to build up as it allows for adding members who identify with your cause or idea. It further allows its members to add their friends and so on. I've found groups to be more interactive as they allow for content sharing amongst members, thus helping you grow your follower base. The business page is not as interactive and is not as easy to grow. I'm sure some have encountered a problem where you invite all of your friends to "like" your page and only a few respond. More will join as your organization grows, but people treat "likes" as if they are "currency" and they will make you work for it. Since the fan base of the page is harder to grow your message will take time to spread. Social media platforms like Facebook, while they have made marketing easier, they have their bottom line to look after. Hence, if you want to reach a larger audience pool, you will most likely have to shell out a few shekels or hire a marketer to help you. I find it more effective to use both the group and page to deliver my message.

A few tips for social media success—in order to keep growing either your group or page, you must not allow them to get stale. New content that offers an everyday "practical value" should be added frequently in order to keep your fans and followers interested.

Social media marketing should not be the only marketing tool you rely on. A successful organization or business ensures that they communicate with a wide audience base. Hence, e-mail marketing is an essential tool to utilize on a continuing basis. One of the best ways to build up a professional relationship with your followers is to continue staying in touch with them and to offer them the everyday "practical value" that will keep them coming back for more. Speaking of value, in order to continuously build your e-mailing list, it is imperative to create campaigns that offer people an incentive to share their e-mails with you. The better the value, the higher the probability that people will share. Furthermore, I would advise creating a newsletter in order to continue building rapport with your supporter base. Thorough research would help you to select the best e-mail marketing platforms for your needs. Not all platforms are created equal. Talk to a marketing professional for ideas on how to build a marketing campaign that would deliver measurable results that would propel you forward.

"ESTABLISHING IDENTITY" - PRINTING AND DESIGN

No organization should be taken seriously without investing funds into creating its own uniquely identifiable brand. As the saying goes, "You only get one chance to make a first impression." Your investment plays a crucial role in helping you create the right kind of impression. When I meet with a professional, I look for specific characteristics to identify whether this person would be a good fit for me. Those characteristics are how they present themselves and if they take their business seriously. Imagine meeting a professional who shakes your hand and presents you with cheaply designed and/or poorly printed business cards, or worse, one that looks just like a business card you saw from a cleaning service. Now consider that this professional will handle your finances or your legal affairs. If mentioned person cannot afford a professionally design and or printed product, it could mean that either they do not take themselves seriously or are not successful.

Hence, it is essential for you to work with a professional graphic artist and a printer. If this professional also understands marketing, you are all set. It would benefit you if all of those services are offered at the same company. When our media company works with a client, we do not just recommend the most appropriate design. We also pair it up with the most appropriate print product and ensure they are making their best impression. I cannot begin to tell you how many times a client would work with an inexperienced designer just to save some money and then would discover that they have to invest more money just to receive their expected result. While bargain shopping may seem to be a good idea, it may end up costing you more in the long run. Make the right kind of impression, the first time—all the time!

MEDIA & PR

While social media has become one of the most effective modes of getting your message across, one should not overlook all the benefits of engaging traditional media outlets. I have found that your local media can play an important role in enabling you to reach your target audience and aid in creating a brand identity. Furthermore, media offers you a vital opportunity to build your organization's credibility. Publishing an article about your organization's activity helps readers begin building a connection as they learn more about what you do and why your organization should be supported.

There are a number of avenues one should consider pursuing to engage media. The simplest, albeit more expensive route, is to hire a public relations specialist who has an existing relationship with the media. This option, while effective, can also be costly. Another alternative is to do it yourself. Assuming that you follow the basic steps of how to create an effective and poignant press release and then how to disseminate it to relevant media outlets, there is no guarantee that you would be able to secure desired coverage. Many times, established professional relationships with local media and bloggers can produce the sought-after results more effectively.

A FEW PARTING WORDS

As I wrap up, I cannot help but wonder what world-changing initiatives would materialize within the next few years. My goal was to compact seven key topics that each, rightfully, command their own chapters if not books. I cannot stress the importance of heeding my advice of creating strategic alliances. Moreover, do not discount the importance of being an educated user of social media and e-mailing resources. Additionally, recall where I discussed the importance of investing in print collateral and working with experienced professionals. Periodically, I encounter people who initially hire novices based on the affordability factor and then end up hiring a professional after the project goes south. Finally, remember the importance of working with media and generating vital PR for your organization. I cannot stress enough the importance of building relationships with media to help you secure necessary coverage.

Many of us, as entrepreneurs, dream of leaving a lasting footprint that would drive change and positively impact the future generations. It is through entrepreneurship that ideas bear fruit. Our greatest foe is doubting ourselves—it is the deterrence that assures the slaying of our dreams.

The idea is the first step to the realization of our goals, but your idea, without perseverance and strategic planning, is merely an unfulfilled idea.

ABOUT LEONARD

Leonard Mogul is a community advocate, distinguished media personality and market development director with Kontinent Media Group. Founder of Arts4Kids Foundation, he is a prolific advocate for his community with a focus on community advocacy, PR, market development and philanthropy.

For those seeking guidance, please write to:
Leonard.Mogul@mail.com.

KNOWING WHEN FAITH, FAILURE, AND YOUR BEHAVIOR LEADS TO YOUR SUCCESS

by Pierre DeBois

It's hard to put into words what entrepreneurs should learn from other entrepreneurs. There are a lot of concepts and tactics that go into a business. To be honest, the search for meaningful guidance can feel never ending.

Well, I hope with this chapter I can make your search less overwhelming.

My company, Zimana, offers analytics consultancy to businesses to investigate the right marketing and business strategy. For the past ten years, Zimana has worked with businesses of varying size and scale on their digital marketing, reviewing relevant website data and results from their social media, paid search, and SEO efforts. Moving forward, Zimana has begun to pivot towards advanced analytics services using R programming to provide analysis. Zimana is the first minority-owned firm with digital analytics as its core service offerings.

My purpose in this chapter is to focus on information that helps you, the reader, operate your business for the long haul. Staying focused consumes personal and financial resources but keeping alert for business solutions is essential for making entrepreneurship really work for you—rather than becoming an expensive hobby.

That alertness is at the heart of faith. Whether you are a devoted evangelical, a traditional Baptist, a quiet Episcopalian, an atheist, a Buddhist, Muslim, practicing spirituality, or just on a journey of self-discovery, you express your faith as a strong belief of how the world works, and you make decisions with an expectation that those actions are working out according to a larger nebulous good in the world.

But actions of faith are not necessarily actions of ethics. It is possible for someone to quote scripture and still act unethically. You must have an ethical self-awareness—the version of you that understands when actions can become unethical. Ethical self-awareness comes from an ongoing scrutiny of actions against standards without romanticizing your role or the ideas behind that action. Loyalty. Love. Faith. All are great ideas that sometimes are applied in distorted ways to take advantage of people.

Having ethical self-awareness is difficult to maintain in a business setting. However, an ethical self-awareness is essential for establishing trust as well as expertise. Bringing forth an ethical sensibility in your actions can come from a solid faith in yourself that you are doing the right thing. But that faith is not always easy to enact. The most ethical people can make unethical choices from time to time. Conditions behind the reason for an ethical change can shift—without notice or warning. A relentless overemphasis on achieving goals overlooks those conditions, creating a narrow vision at the expense of other factors that can be important.

Being a leader means you are held to a higher standard, being vigilant on how others view your intentions—even when the actions taken are well intended. Look at your actions without romanticizing an idea around meaningless dogma.

To consider how ethical you are, seek activities that allow you to assess critical moments that come to mind. Spend time journaling or talking to a good advisor to get to the root of what you are facing. If you are unsure how to approach people involved in a situation, level-set with those people to clear as much air as possible. Keep in mind, psychological safety is absolutely needed to speak out on issues—the absence of that safety is sometimes why people don't come forth with what they are thinking.

If people are not allowing that safety to exist—to let ethical behavior exist in a given situation—then be ready to leave them and the unethical situation behind.

Every now and then take in every accomplishment and ask yourself, "Is a customer or client better because of my involvement?" whether that involvement is a product or service.

When you ask that question—and if you are in your first few years, ignore the revenue numbers. Sometimes you need to know if you are making a difference, especially if mistakes with customers have occurred.

If you can't name what that improvement is in a sentence or two, there's a problem. You're not necessarily on the road to bankruptcy, but you can mismanage your business by not having a story to share with potential customers about how your product or service successfully helped someone. That story is what a potential customer must hear in their consideration of using your services. It's what they want to hear.

The story must be an honest one, not one that stretches the truth into an outright lie to customers and partners.

The first two years in operation make such a story hard to establish. If you can't answer it within 2 years, give yourself a bit of a break. It takes time to explain how people are benefiting from your offering.

But after 2 years if you can't name what you did for a customer or client that led to a sale, make no doubt...you ARE in trouble.

Another assessment involves how you work with people. I've seen more than a few people complain about friends and family not supporting their business. Sometimes the gripes are legit—people close to you can act toxic and create disruption. Small business teams usually consist of a few people, leaving no room for personal drama. Drama is like catching a cold; when one person catches it, the team catches it, and the whole business is sick.

You should be cautious on criticizing the support friends and family offer to your business. Not everyone can support you with a purchase or referral at the time you need it. Sometimes friends can show support in other, better ways, like taking your kids regularly to soccer when you have a 2-month long project that eats into personal time. Having faith in people sometimes means taking a step back from requesting a favor from the task you wanted the most. It is also a show of faith that the right resources will come to you in time. That one best friend, even a great one, may not be the right resource at the given moment. When it comes to your business you have to trust God, Allah, and the fates to pull the right moments beyond your control together.

Moreover, your marketing strategy is what sustains your attraction to customers. If you are starting out, you should work to establish a strategy first. Overreliance on immediate contacts is the major reason why Multi-Level Marketing (MLM) models are not terrific business choices. A business model is EXACTLY how your business earns income. An MLM business model usually overemphasizes sales percentages based upon how many people join your "biz". A group of people together in a pyramid is a financial overhead that runs counter to long-term profitability.

The right decision is to pick your customer markets with care. **If your idea failed to attract sales, it's because it didn't solve an important problem for a large number of people in your market. Full stop.**

Most advice for business success consists of phrases and concepts—"Market your business consistently"; "Watch your cash flow", and others. While many of these are indeed true, the reality is your business success will be based on how several ideas, not one or two, are implemented and managed together.

In short, beware of trite advice you receive. Instead you need real domain knowledge applied to that advice for your situation. Game changers come from specific concepts and tools applied to how you and your team operate, not suggestions that do not fit your operations or cost you capital. If someone is giving advice, ask for the research behind it or what details are being observed that created the advice.

The same idea holds for motivation memes with trite sayings. Real motivation is based on altering your world, or at least taking the steps to do so. Memes are sometimes a temporary emotional fix that just speak to self-worth. They feel shallow because they don't focus on solving customer problems. Make sure your inspirations come from meaningful work, not shallow work. Shallow activity never adds up to much.

Don't get me wrong. Being positive can be a good first gear to get you moving into your day, but over time you must assess what is really getting accomplished in your business.

Say "No" to people reasonably, even if the way you are being asked a favor is an annoyance to you. Most people, in my experience, have been cool. But there have been a few times when people have asked for too much, when the request could have been made to someone else or the answer to the request could have been handled with a Google query.

Remaining gracious is part of the territory with business leadership. Doing so reflects picking your battles with wisdom, particularly with friends and people with close ties. Most folks are not trying to set off an argument, so in many instances, let people know reasonably why you have preferences against something, and then see if they respond, rather than give a snarky response. Not everyone is trying to ruin your schedule, and even if the comment presents a "cray-cray" logic, you can sometimes go further in your day by avoiding an over-the-top reply.

Learning how to create content for your business is a terrific way to assess where you are going. Content is just a fancy-schmancy way of describing email notes, blogs, videos, and podcasts—any media that you produce for your business.

You won't have enough time to pitch every person, so your content should fill those gaps. Your content should tell a brief story of what your business provides and how it addresses your customer's needs. It's ok if not every piece is picture perfect, but you do need to have content organized to show how you work with people in real life and listen to customer needs carefully.

Maintaining mental health—defined as your emotional psychological and social well-being - is becoming a way overdue discussion in entrepreneurship circles. The grind of starting a business and keeping it going can drain emotional stamina.

Keep in mind you can experience mental health issues at various points in your lifetime, but they are not a deal breaker for running a business. Any part of the body can get ill, including the mind.

You should manage your life so that you can stay alert for potential mental health issues in others and yourself, such as eating or sleeping too little, severe mood swings, consistently avoiding people who consider close relationships, or an increase in frequency of smoking, drinking or using drugs. An inability to get tasks done results from high anxiety, avoidance, job disinterest, and a dramatic loss in personal energy—all of which can ruin a good business and impact the people who network and partner with you.

Developing positive coping skills is critical to keeping mental health issues manageable. It means selecting activities that induce positive moods—not just giving yourself a fake, toxic "be-happy-always" message. Seek physical activity in your spare time, help others, or develop the skills relevant to your business. Your anxiety will disappear—at least for a little while—and you will start to feel the real positive sentiment you need to move ahead.

Find the right platform for raising your company's exposure to customers. The success of Amazon, and its influence on retail and tech, has created an environment where not having the right exposure cripples your company. But a platform does not have to be for retail. If you operate in a B2B market, assess your network and ask what impact it is having on meaningful referrals and sales. Always question the value of an ongoing association over time.

Make great referrals for partners and others. Be knowledgeable about a person's firm so that you know when a given referral is potentially worthwhile. I always call people to make sure a referral has worked out, and I think twice to refer people who were extremely dishonest in the past or did nothing.

Vetting referrals can protect your cash flow, especially if your business works with Business-to-Business (B2B) markets. Just like a bank trusts a buyer to make new car payments for 5-7 years, you are trusting referred B2B clients to become customers who can pay for your products and services. The success of your business is measured in cash flow. The faith you have in how you vet customers impact that cash flow.

You have to be a little bold and share the merits of your business and offerings at many opportunities. That's the nature of the game. But the biggest mistake I see from small businesses is to just get on social media and post a lot of "buy now" or "see us now" messages—and nothing else. That kind of decision-making is unwise, yet understandable. Social media posting costs nothing. It's too easy to post a series of messages that says the same thing "buy now".

Social media algorithms have changed a lot, especially after the 2016 U.S. elections. You need to plan your marketing across a number of media platforms, with different kinds of messaging as a reminder of your value to customers. It can draw the right customers, who will do business with you repeatedly and send the right referrals. Word of mouth is still valuable, but you should tailor your message to different moments in the customer's purchase consideration.

Being capable across a number of skillsets requires you to be incredibly messy for a while. The messiness is the source of many failures in business and life. The reality is that you have to practice a few things to get the right things for your customers. Be appreciative of the journey necessary to get those skillsets right. It will show how faith and failure informs your success.

I hope I have given you one more set of ideas that you want to share with someone else.

ABOUT PIERRE

As founder & CEO of Zimana, Pierre has developed talents and insights that have served small businesses and large enterprises on analytics and business strategy. Zimana reviews data from digital analytics and social media dashboard solutions for improvements in marketing, Web development, and business operations.

Pierre has also established himself as an analytics and business intelligence writer. He has contributed a variety of digital analytics and marketing articles for *CMS Wire, Information Week, DMNews*, and several publications on *Medium*. He has also been an associate editor of business book reviews for Small Business Trends since 2010.

In addition, Pierre has lead specialty projects such as being a technical editor for Pearson/Que Publications. He consulted on books authored by Ramon Ray (The Small Business Guide To Facebook Marketing) and Marcus Hammonds (God, Technology, and Us)

Pierre holds a mechanical engineering degree from Prairie View A&M and an MBA from Georgia Tech. His background in business and engineering include Ford Motor Co. and Lesco, a minority-owned government logistics contractor.

He is a native of Gary, Indiana, serving the Chicago area and beyond.

Pierre can be contacted at www.zimana.com and on Linked In.

MORE ON SUCCESS

Success is igniting the power of your spirit, through your faith, so that you can continuously do better and your presence on this earth serves to uplift others.

–Jennifer Christenson

Success has many meanings and is defined differently by everyone. It's the journey and not the destination. While on the journey, there will be ups and downs, so it's necessary to gather tools or lessons that help clear your pathway. Success is having faith that your failures are your successes and play a contributing factor in making your life meaningful on your terms, as defined by you and not others. So, it's important to have a "never give up mindset" if you plan to accomplish anything in life.

—Robert Hazzard

Success, for me, isn't necessarily measured by the title you hold, your social status, material possessions, or how much money you have in your bank account, but rather being able to reflect on your life and know that you have been the best version of yourself possible and have utilized your God-given talents to impact the lives of others for the better.

–Connie Glover

Success is not measured in dollars or collections or accomplishments. Success is measured in time. Do you have the time to do the things you really want to do? Some people are fortunate to get paid to do what they love. That is a kind of success, but most people don't get that. For the rest, they have to figure out what it is they really love to do, and make time for that in their lives. The person who loves to paint and has plenty of time for painting, but has a modest day job and a small home, is more of a success than the millionaire with a huge home who never gets to relax there. The person who enjoys the simple things and lives longer for lack of stress is more of a success than the billionaire who dies young of a heart attack. I urge you to really think about how you define success before you rush off and try to be a success by someone else's definition!

—James L. Papandrea, M.Div., Ph.D.

Success is different for everyone, and in different phases of your life, it will mean different things...Success is knowing that the greatest work of your life will be digging deep to understand why you are the way you are and why you do the things you do. Success is breaking out of generational patterns, committing to your growth, having the courage to heal, build, and to create. Success is learning how to be present and at peace amidst the chaos because you have faith in God, who will never leave you. Success is growing to learn and truly feel that validation, peace, safety, and love will never be found in others before it is found within you, where your faith in God resides. Success is operating from a place of gratitude because you realize that because of your faith, you do not have to fear failure...it is trusting that your faith will set you free.

—Jennifer Christenson

Success is looking at oneself in the mirror, proud in knowing that you had the courage to give your very best today and that each day we are evolving to become the highest version of ourselves. It's knowing that, today and every day, we took action in a positive direction despite how challenging it might have been, because these actions make way for others on their journey. Others' successes, growth and happiness are our own because we are all one.

—Tangee Moscoso

The greatest success is a PEACE OF MIND. Most people have equated "success" with wealth, money and materialistic gain. In most cases, those people are suffering due to the pressures of life that come with trying to live an UNREALISTIC life. So, once again, my success is my PEACE OF MIND!!!

—Cortez Mack

Success means different things to different people. For many, success is measured by material acquisitions. I used to tie success to a dollar amount, but now, success is being able to do what I enjoy doing and pursuing my calling in life. Success is having the freedom to manage my time to use the gifts God has given me without restraints. I won't put a price tag on what it costs to be a success, but the power of feeling like a success is priceless.

—Anthony Ellis McGee

Success means that I have accomplished what I worked so hard for. If I've put in effort and worked hard for what I wanted to achieve, then I feel that I have accomplished my goals. It's a high achievement when you can say that you completed a task or goal!

—Mona McIlwain

Success means to me that I've effectively achieved the goals that I've set out to accomplish. This can be in the form of dreams coming into fruition, overcoming difficult challenges, and/or executing greatness as defined by me. In my life, I've found that there hasn' been just one specific path to success. However, I know that it doe: involve a few key elements such as aligned passion, drive, har work, sacrifice and timing - all sprinkled with a bit of faith on top.

—Shari C. Hill , MBA, MHRN

Success is accomplishing what you set out to do and doing it th best that you are able to do. It is also exceeding the expectations setting high goals and achieving them. Success is being able t influence others around you to lead them to their own successes.

—Mary Stowers, Cancer Survivo

Success to me is a little different than it is to others. My success i being able to offer others hope through their struggles. My succes: is when I get a call or message from someone that says, "Tamm because of you I didn't give up!!"

—Tammy Lyn Connor:

CPSIA information can be obtained
at www.ICGtesting.com
Printed in the USA
FSHW010646160221